WILDFLOWER

From Wicked to Warrior

This book is dedicated to my Pops, Mike Lee,

Who inspired me to share my story.

My mentor. My best friend.

THANK YOU, POPS.

Also, to my Moms, Sharon,

Who just let me be a kid...

And Deb... thank you for being my Sweesta.

And a shout-out to my New Life family.

I LOVE YOU ALL.

This book is written like none other. It is NOT grammatically correct or punctuation-perfect. But it is poured out from my heart to yours. It is of me, for you. And all of it is true.

It is for the alcoholic, the addict, the depressed.
It is for the broken, the lost, and the hopeless.

Table of Contents

CHAPTER 1

MEMORIES

Imagine this:

A white wall. An old brown recliner. A little blonde-haired girl, age unknown, sitting in the middle of a house filled with rage! Yelling and screaming coming from the angry mouth of a drunken mother. The disgusting smells of cigarettes and cheap whiskey fill the room. An absolutely terrifying and unwanted place to be!

Then suddenly, with extreme anger, these stinky, yellow-stained hands grab the front of this child's shirt and throw her tiny body against that white wall! Leaving this child to crumble to the floor. In pain. Confused. Crying but hiding the tears. Completely terrified and careful not to "poke the bear" any further. No need to push buttons for further hostilities.

This child was... ME.

Let me introduce myself. My name is Terri. Well, at least it used to be. I will explain that later. I was Terri, the Terrific, or Terri, the Terrible. Terribly Terrific... for 50 years.

My real name is Terese. I didn't find my way back to the beauty of that name until much later in my life. Once again, I will explain all that during my final chapters. Stay tuned. It's really good stuff. Anyway, I lived in a place controlled by alcohol and abuse—physical, mental, and sexual. A nightmare.

Imagine the very worst, then multiply those thoughts by 10. Then do that again. Certainly not a place for a child to blossom.

My "home" consisted of my younger brother (I will call him Howie), my abusive, drunken mother, "Rowdy," and myself. I put quotations around the word "home" because it was not much of a "home." It never was... no matter where we lived. My mother never paid any of the bills—rent, power, water, etc.—so she would change her name, move to another dump (sometimes with no power or maybe no running water, which meant no toilet, too!), and then eventually, she would be served with an eviction notice.

It was habitual to receive those notices—a normal practice, like a piece of everyday mail. We would move, then move again, and then move some more. Finally, I just stopped unpacking. Be ready for the next time. No stability there. A constant whirlwind of chaos.

There were days and days that my brother and I would go without food. Whatever money there was went towards booze and cigarettes—Rowdy's devices. Her only goal was to have no goals. Back then, we had milkmen delivering milk and eggs to paying households. We were not one of those places, unfortunately.

Three days had passed, and our tummies were howling at us. Excruciating and painful, I had to do something. So, I chased down the neighborhood milkman and begged him for food—literally. Crying my little eyes out, snot running down my chin, I got the bad news.

He told me that he could not help; he was on his route, and then he drove away. But within an hour, a miracle took place! This milkman was at our gate with groceries—milk, eggs, potatoes, and even bread! We were blessed with such great gifts!

I thanked him and ran inside to feed my little brother. Grateful. The second memory I can recall? Age 7. Tender years. A little blonde-haired baby girl with hazel green eyes, learning about survival.

My "family" and I were getting ready to move from our tiny, three-street town to a much larger area. The city had so much to offer. There were so many people, everyone busy, living their comfortable lives. Heck, this city even had stoplights, unlike my hometown, which had none. We were so invisible.

So, my hometown consisted of three bars, no grocery store, and a three-room schoolhouse (one room held kindergarten, first grade, and second grade; then 3rd, 4th, and 5th in another room, followed by 6th, 7th, and 8th grade in the last room). Everyone knew everyone. But no one helped anyone. All for one and one for all. A very selfish place to be. Secrets STAYED secret. Period.

During our move, Tiger, my mother's cat, ran away. And it was MY responsibility to go find her. Since I was unable to locate Tiger, I was left behind with the next-door neighbors. I didn't want to stay there, but I knew I had no say in the matter. As Rowdy packed the last boxes into the forest service green Suburban, she turned to me and said,

"If you don't find Tiger, I won't come back for you."

She then drove 45 miles away, abandoning me. My 7-year-old self was horrified. Scared to death. Why would my mom just leave me? I know she doesn't like me... but this? This wasn't fair. It wasn't nice. Just NOT right. Left with strangers. His name was Dave. (Maybe that's why I don't care for that name... Hmmm) His wife's name? Unimportant. Wicked people. Very wicked people. Disgusting, vile humans.

Bedtime came. I was forced into the only bedroom that existed, which belonged to them. You could smell the evil and feel the darkness in the room. Odors of mold and mildew, old and stale. A gross stench. There seemed to be some sort of cloud that hovered inside the room. It was so heavy.

A deep, deep sense of gloom crept in without any welcoming. And then it happened. Cold, wet fingers touching me. Then, touching himself. Touching places I didn't even know I had. So confused and utterly terrified. I closed my eyes in that darkness and pretended to be anywhere else. Anywhere but there.

I saw a flowing waterfall rippling with vivid blue and white colors. I could feel the coolness of the water and hear the roaring of its magnificence. In the foreground, swaying wheat-long grass, gold in color, and the smell of the sweet earth. I pictured myself slowly walking through the grass; it touched me softly, like a loving kiss. I was invited in. I made it to this glorious water. I plunged into it. It was so refreshing. I swam to the waterfall. I found peace.

This is *MY SAFE PLACE. MY WATERFALL.* But the nightmare continued. Those wicked, evil people assaulted a 7-year-old baby girl. Molested her sexually. No need for too many more details, but it was truly ugly. I was just a child. They raped me of my innocence. They stole it. Like thieves. Sexual predators preying on the weak.

My world was now forever changed...Welcome to Hell.

It's no coincidence; this was also the year I started my relationship with alcohol. Miller high life ponies and I became the best of "buds." They were mid-sized beers, but nonetheless, very potent for a kid. Rowdy would have belligerent house parties with her drunken buddies, and I was always the bartender, the singer, her entertainment.

It's no wonder that I spent the next 47 years being best friends with booze. YES, 47 YEARS! That's a very long time when you really think about it. I had no real preference when it came to my alcohol. Beer, whiskey, shots, shooters. Light it on fire, pour it in someone's belly button, or straight off the bar. It didn't matter. Just pour it in.

Get it down. My sickening search for it was a constant daily plan. Every single day. Without fail.

Every morning, my first thought was ALWAYS how to achieve the next buzz. The next drunk. I could find the party or be the party. I was very skilled at finding the "all-nighters." Those are the parties that close down the bars at 2 a.m. and rage into the morning hours. I found that one way to cure a hangover is to just keep drinking.

Through the night and into the morning, I would start again, which usually involved lots of puking. I would say over and over how it was a good thing because I made room for more. It was pathetic. Disgusting. I knew it was a terrible way to live, but it's all that I knew. That is how you live, right?

Fast forward two years, age 9. That little blonde-haired girl was now adjusting to the wickedness of this real world. The big city we lived in brought its own share of problems, that's for sure. How could it not? If it existed in that tiny little town, how could it not be even worse there?

Let me tell you what I have learned: evil lurks everywhere. Every nook and cranny. Every city and every town. Every state and country. You don't have to look very far to witness any of it. It is right before your eyes.

It is this world. Horrifying. So, once again, Rowdy was "in need" of her devices: her crutches, whiskey, and cigs! The monthly welfare money ran out, and now it was time for a "trade." She usually sold her food stamps to someone, but this time, she did not. Maybe she ran out of those for the month, too.

Anyway, I was forced to "stay" with the neighbors, Larry and Naomi, who lived two doors down. I still can't forget them. I see them as dark shadows in my mind now. They were very bad people.

Bad. Bad. Bad. I knew that my mother had made some sort of deal with them. It was not a good deal for me.

She had "traded" me for a bottle of whiskey. More than likely, she scored cigarettes, as well. I didn't understand it! And I still don't. Who gives away their child to unknown people? Especially not being aware of the evil inside. Who? My mom, that's who.

Evil lies EVERYWHERE!

Although what was happening was extremely disgusting and wrong, I think that the sickest part of all of it was the fact that his wife, Naomi, KNEW. She watched. She allowed it to happen. Her eyes appeared to be as red as the devil as she stood on her staircase. Watching. Sickening. He opened his robe and gestured for me to "come sit" between his hairy man legs.

I did what I thought I was supposed to. He brushed my hair and disrobed completely. I felt him against my back. I froze. Tried to be invisible. Afraid. Don't move, and maybe it'll all go away.

Another visit to hell. It seems to greet me with a snarly growl, "Welcome back!"

So, I traveled inside my head to *MY WATERFALL*. *MY SAFE PLACE*. Wish I could stay there. Forever. Eventually, ... "it" went away.

Years later, upon turning 14, this was the year I became much wiser about the world. My discoveries led me to believe that this earthly domain was (and still is) a truly wicked place. I really didn't have much for friends. No trust in anyone. Blonde tomboy, running around, trying to fit in. Hanging out with my baby brother mostly. And when I wasn't taking on the role of "mother" for him, we were busy escaping by riding 3-wheelers and motorcycles off into the sunset. Well, at least as far as half a tank of gas would get us.

Knowing we had to turn around and head back towards the emptiness we ran away from.

Rowdy was always in the bars, drowning herself with booze, so that meant we were left unattended on a very regular basis. We had to fend for ourselves. Whether it was to find food, go to school, do our homework, or even hand wash our own clothes, that's what we did. We stayed out of the way and just barely existed. I almost think that it was the "norm" back then. I remember days of not eating, no food in the house. The hunger pains that screamed out, only to be ignored. Wondering why there was always enough money for alcohol but never enough for nourishment. Forgotten children. Abandoned children.

Then, one day, it all changed. My one and only male friend, Don (name changed, of course), did what my mother had told him to do. She had given him a bottle of Jack Daniels and a $5 bill and ordered him to take my virginity. Yes, I stated that correctly.

He was to steal what was left of my innocence. Make me a woman. Maybe Rowdy thought her parental duties would come to an end. I honestly do not know. What makes a person think such deranged thoughts? And what kind of person acts on those ideas? Well, my mom fit right into both disturbing questions. I feel sadness in my heart for her. Strange!

Rowdy had shared with me that it was a personal rite of passage for a mother to betray her daughter in a very horrific way. Apparently, my grandmother had done the same thing to her. Hmmmm... I don't think that is hereditary. Correct me if I am wrong. It's not in someone's genes to be cruel like that! It's in the evil choices they make. A choice that destroys.

I tried running away so many times. I needed to escape the torture that ran wild in my life. And I got caught every single time. I was placed in six different foster homes and one group home. These places were NO better than where I just ran from. Most of these "parents" were only in it for the monthly payments they received. It wasn't to better that child, that's for sure!

Abuse followed by more abuse. Physical, sexual, and mental. All forms of abuse. Saddening! And in those days, no one was ever investigated. Swept under the carpet. Hush Hush. Give them their monthly allotment. And now it's no longer the state's problem. Or the birth parents. NO fixing. Jus failing.

A child lost. Many children were lost.

CHAPTER 2

The KILLINGS

7 DEATHS. 7 KILLINGS. From jealousy. From hatred. Rowdy was never appreciative of the love I displayed towards anything or anyone. My love was supposed to go towards her and her alone. I just couldn't understand how I was supposed to love a monster. Even if it was my own flesh and blood! How? Her anger became evil. Evil. So disturbing, it still haunts me today.

Duchess was a German Shepherd dog I once knew. She was my everything. My best friend. My confidant. My partner. I had no friends since I could NOT bring anyone home. What kind of shape would my mother (I use that term "mother" very loosely!) be in? Would she be tipsy? Would she be three sheets to the wind? Would she be angry? Would she be passed out? Never knowing the outcome, I just avoided it altogether. It was best that way.

Anyway, I recall being on a swing at a park down the street from my house with my faithful and loyal dog by my side. Another child had come close to me, and apparently, my mother saw this interaction. I'm not too sure what was going on in her mind, but when I returned later that day from school, my dog was missing, unlike her.

I searched and searched and found her nowhere. Hours passed, and my tears were still drenching my face. Then I heard the truth: Rowdy had killed her. She said she witnessed my furry friend attacking that child earlier. False. So she "rid me of her," and I was to "get over it!"

That was killing number 1. How wicked eyes can be when viewing through a whiskey bottle. The second and third killings were just as cruel. Freedom and Daisy. Two Saint Bernard dogs. Daisy was the female pup for me, and the male pup, Freedom, was for my little brother. I don't remember much about them because they didn't last long. Once again, my mom had become enraged that love was directed towards animals and not herself.

It was a school day in that tiny little town, mid-afternoon, when my mom informed the schoolhouse and teachers that a vicious dog was on the loose. She suggested everyone "hunker down" and not go outside. Protect yourselves from the mad beast running through town! We did. No one went outside. And then we discovered the "mad dog" that was running was Freedom, my brother's pet.

The next words were, "No worries! It's being taken care of," with a sense of calmness.

My mother really was a Dr. Jekyll and Mr. Hyde. She had asked the neighbor to take this "nasty" creature to the hills and discard it. He did. Shot him. My mother was in one of her drunken rages when this happened. The dog did nothing to warrant his death. She hated the love we had for him.

Shortly afterward, it was Daisy's turn to be executed. She was doing her "dog thing" and roaming around. Back then, that's what every owner did. They were not kept in yards or on leashes. They just roamed. Daisy came home after being hit by a car. In bad shape— part of her face was missing, bloody, and furless. Some skull was showing. I really thought she could have been saved. Maybe not, but I am still convinced her death was unnecessary. Rowdy would have no discussion of this matter. Absolutely none. Her decision was final. "End of story."

Daisy would be terminated. Say your goodbyes. I did. That was killing numbers 2 and 3. The next murders are horrifying. Something I still try not to think about. I wish there was a way to erase the images from my head, but they are vivid, just as they were that day. Oreo and Sylvester. Two black and white kitties, siblings. One for me, one for my sibling. How awesome, right? It WAS.

These two cats did everything with us. Literally EVERYTHING! They took walks with us, went hiking way up in the mountains, slept, ate, and even bathed with us! As a matter of fact, we had a little pond out back. We used rubber inner tubes for floating, and those kitties would ride along on top! It was crazy and awesome!

For those who don't know, CATS HATE WATER. They would also sit on the front porch and faithfully wait for the school bus to arrive. That big yellow can hold their favorite people inside. It was always a warm, fuzzy, and loving welcome. We looked forward to it. So, when they weren't there, we KNEW what had happened.

We searched and searched. And then we searched some more. All our hiking trails, the pond out back, the road we walked down daily — everywhere. No ground was left untouched. Then, when we woke up, the search started again. Our voices became hoarse from calling their names.

"OREO," "SYLVESTER," "KITTY, KITTY"

"Please come back."

We couldn't face the obvious. Was there a killer on the loose again? Weeks turned into months. We never gave up hope. They were family to us. About four months went by. Our mother still insisted that they "must have run away!" but never answered our one question: "At the same time?" How odd. And untrue. She looked like deceit. Smelled of it. It went well with her whiskey breath and cigarette stench. Great combo.

We found them. We usually stayed outdoors, away from the devil inside. While playing out back by the pond, we noticed some straw bales in a very weird spot. Our curiosity took over. Why were they there? What was their purpose? Let's go look!

A cellar! WOW! How did we not know it was there? It was attached to the back of the shack we were living in. The door was swollen, and we struggled to open it. It slammed open. We kept investigating. Onward, young children! Another discovery at hand! A burlap gunny sack. And it was heavy!

We struck gold! There MUST be treasures inside! Why else would it be here, hidden from the world? Oreo. Sylvester. Dead. Trapped in a sack. Eyes still open. TERRIFIED. She had drowned them in our favorite spot, the pond, and then threw them away.

My heart cries. My face flooded with tears. Then and now. Killings 4 and 5. The last killings are truly sad to think about. No child should be aware of such tragedies. Ever. I want to believe my mother felt some sort of guilt because shortly after the devastation of the last murders, she had two presents waiting for us when we returned home from school one day.

We stepped off the bus and onto the porch, where two dogs anxiously wagged their tails and jumped excitedly. Blackie and Red. How original with the names, right? I was told Blackie was a French Shepherd, very much like a German Shepherd, but only black in color. To this day, I'm not sure if that is truly a breed. And no, I haven't googled it yet.

It didn't matter because I fell in love with him instantly. He was mine. Red was an Irish Setter, and my brother was ecstatic to have him. It seemed these two dogs had grown up together. They were inseparable. Their relationship reminded me of Howie and me. Inseparable. Close.

One evening, we noticed our dogs were acting very strange. Whining, wincing in pain. Upon discovery, they had been attacked by a porcupine. WHEW! Our thoughts led us to believe it was "HER" again—the "MURDERER." She had done something. AGAIN. Thankfully, we were wrong.

Pulling porcupine quills from a dog's snout is NOT an easy task. They growl, they snap at you, and they even bite you. Yes, the hand that feeds them becomes their enemy. At last, success! Practicing to be a veterinarian wasn't such a difficult thing. Mission accomplished. The dogs were happy, and so were we. All was good. Or was it?

It seemed to be a theme with Rowdy that things would be drastically different when we got home from school. We dreaded it. No dogs anywhere. They were gone. Rowdy told us that an infection had taken over, and there was nothing anyone could do. They needed to be "put down immediately." Arguments ensued. Unanswered doubts. Anger. Hatred. Betrayal. Confusion. Sadness. So many emotions. Ignored.

That was the last of the killings. The murders. And there were no more pets.

CHAPTER 3

THE OTHER ALCOHOLIC

This is the section where I need to share a little bit about my dad—the other alcoholic. There is not much to tell because I didn't know him.

My mother, brother, and I lived in a two-story yellow house in a mediocre town. We kids were playing outside, and I was pretending to be my brother's dog, so I wore a leash and hung out in the doghouse.

Then, suddenly, we heard, "Your f****** dad's coming!" It was our mom, yelling at us with her trashy mouth.

What? What dad? We didn't know about any dad! What did she mean? So much confusion stirred in our little heads. There was never any mention of our dad or even his existence. And in all actuality, we didn't question his whereabouts. Why would we? Absence is bliss, or so I'm told.

Pulling up in front of our house was a wood-paneled, reddish-brown station wagon. Stepping out was an old, gray-haired man. Apparently, this was our sperm donor—our dad. Yay. The stench of alcohol permeated his entire being, so we went on with our playtime, ignoring him, just as he had ignored us all our lives. The only question was: why was he even here? We will discover the answer to that question later.

Several days went by, and they just continued their drunken, buzzed-up time. Buddy-buddies. Best friends when alcohol was involved. Drink, then fight. Drink, then fight. Soon afterwards, I was forced to give up my room (which consisted of a single bed on the back porch). It usually stayed cold in there, but at least it was away from my mother. I was forgotten back there, and I was glad.

An "incident" occurred upstairs, and my mom would later admit to what really happened. There were always raging parties upstairs and downstairs as well (birds of a feather flock together!). It was constant. It was normal. It was our lifestyle: a bunch of drunks bouncing back and forth with beer and whiskey in hand, smoking cigarettes and blabbering nonsense. No one had a lick of sense, or at least they weren't displaying it very well. Constant chatter, mindless and meaningless.

Anyway, the upstairs railing that secured the balcony, keeping people from falling off onto the ground below, had been "loosened." Oddly enough, this was the same exact spot where my dad would often lean while drinking and carrying on.

My mom was clearly trying to kill him. Obviously. She never said this was her intention outright, but I remember her words of sabotage: "Well, that didn't work." The frustration on her face only suggested that her murderous ways had returned. She was unsuccessful at that time.

Attempt number two came later. I still see him in my head, sitting on the edge of my bed, watching M.A.S.H. and reeking of intoxication. I recall finding a pair of his poopy underwear next to my bed and thinking. I will never sleep there again. How gross. I would rather stay in the doghouse outside! So, I did, until his departure.

Then, yelling and screaming erupted from the kitchen. We couldn't make out the exact words, but there was anger. A lot of it. She directed us to sit in the front room, across from the flower-printed sofa where my dad had been napping, inebriated, of course. I remember holding my knees tightly to my chest in fear—knowing something was wrong but not knowing what was about to happen. That deep feeling in your gut that says, "RUN!" But you can't.

With storming footsteps and wielding a marble rolling pin, she marched toward that ugly couch. So much anger! She headed toward the man we barely knew as our dad. And then...

She swung! Hitting him in the head repeatedly over and over and over again! His blood sprayed the white walls; it covered his face. His clothes were soaked. She laughed and kept beating him. More blood. Everywhere! Now soaking into the couch! He was covered in his own blood, from head to toe, trying to fight her off, but he couldn't see. Blood filled his eyes. He stumbled around, trying to defend himself, but couldn't.

So we ran as fast as we could. We ran outside, screaming and crying, looking for help, while she continued to laugh, utterly uncaring about what she had just exposed her children to.

He survived. Again. Survived my mother twice. The cops did nothing to her. Back in those days, there were never any consequences. No one cared. A drunken family, it'll work itself out. Or it won't.

Months later, he died in a car accident. It was soon after he left the hospital (and us kids) that he drove off a cliff and died instantly. Rowdy told us he had gone blind in one of his eyes, so in my head, she was guilty of his death. I attributed his blindness to her beating him. He couldn't see where he was going. Driving blind around a corner. And it was her fault.

These were my young thoughts.

CHAPTER 4

SELF DESTRUCT

During the latter part of my 14th year of life, after the loss of my virginity and childhood, I left home. Finally, I was free! Free at last! Wasn't I? Unsure. Occasionally, I would come back, but nothing had changed. It was best to be on my own. I was a broken child. Confused. Unloved. Unwanted. Discarded like yesterday's trash. So, I left that prison sentence behind. No idea how to evolve. I just knew that I needed to.

The best part was that I would no longer be called terrible names like; "whore," "failure," or "you will never amount to anything!" Heck, I was seven years old! What did I know about whores and failures? Or amounting to anything? Absolutely nothing.

But the words that cut like a knife were the ones like, "I wish you would have **NEVER** been born!" Or "I wish I would've had ten boys... **INSTEAD** of you!"... or the powerful statement of "Why can't you just be like your brother?" Words that still sting as if it was a poison dart. Sometimes, I wish there was a delete button. Erase all the ugly stuff. Wouldn't that be nice?

On the bright side, leaving hell meant no more beatings! No more bruises! No more playing Russian roulette with a **VERY** loaded gun! No more hiding under the bed because she is home from the bars and out of control again! No more strange men staring at me with perverse eyes! NO MORE!!! NO MORE! NO MORE! I am free! Or was I? Still unsure.

High school had nothing to offer me. I was in and out, skipping classes and then missing days, which turned into weeks. No one noticed. No one cared. So, eventually, I just stopped going. There were better things to do with my time. Seek numb-minding substances. Erase the pain inside. Stop the broken in my heart. Fourteen and on my own. What a truly terrifying and liberating state of mind. Undecisive and unruly. Outrageous and obliviated.

I bounced around between abandoned houses, gutted-out trailers, and empty, forgotten cars. I slept wherever my head would land for the night. My drunkenness led me to places I am not proud of. At all. I had no future. I had no hope.

I slept in hallways of condemned buildings and would find myself waking up in a state of disgust. Almost always. Waking up in a strange man's bed, not knowing who he was. Or how I got there. Feeling filthy and anxious to flee! Shameful. Disgusting. Less than human. But this is all I knew... Drink. Get drunk. Drink more. Repeat behavior and then hate yourself. Without a doubt, the strongest feeling I carried inside was a very wicked hatred for myself. Daily.

Seems like I escaped hell, only to find another version of it. Drugs and alcohol. And eventually, it led me to sex. This would lead me to a series of bad choices. I would choose men who used and abused me. Not entirely their fault because I allowed it. I think I sought it out, in a sense. To be smacked around and bruised up was normal. That's how life was lived. Right? Wrong. Absolutely wrong.

These partners loved the drinking and drugging world, so they were ideal for me. The bar scenes, the after-closing parties, or running the same circles for drugs. That's who we were. And whatever came along with that, I just had to accept. And as always, with alcohol use comes physical abuse. ALWAYS. It's inevitable.

And sometimes, more than I care to say, that abuse is followed by sexual abuse, as well. This is the life I chose. A life consisting of "wake and bake" (smoking massive amounts of marijuana IMMEDIATELY upon waking up) and "burn and turn" (inhaling meth constantly and then turning around and doing it all over again.) Was this the life I was given?

Well, I thought so. And was I doomed to live it forever? I believed so. Was it true? Or was I looking for an excuse to keep using it? To accept defeat. Give in and give up! I didn't want those options. I wanted more! And eventually, I would change my way of thinking. I suppose that it is better late than never.

CHAPTER 5

GREAT SHAME

This is the section I have been really struggling with, whether to share this with you or not. Do I let you, the reader, into this deep, dark secret of mine? Or do I keep it within never to release? Maybe share it later? The answer is no. This is extremely ugly and shameful. It is a very painful part of me and scary to tell.

But somewhere inside myself, I keep hearing these words: "If I don't reveal, then I will not heal."

So, I am choosing to share. I will tell you that this chapter will be the shortest. My sex life was filled with so many mistakes—choices I am DEFINITELY NOT proud of. The lesson I learned from Rowdy was that if I opened my legs, I would be loved. That's where love comes from. Crude but true. And extremely vulgar, I know. But I believed it. I believed her lies. No other teachings were given.

The biggest example I can offer is the lack of sexual awareness. In all honesty, I was completely oblivious when it came to the process of reproduction and where babies come from. I was not informed of how they were made. I had no clue—none whatsoever. No one ever told me, and I certainly didn't ask. Why would I? Who would take the time to educate me? Isn't that what a mother does? Hmmm... I know it sounds incredibly naive, but at the age of 16, I truly had no idea. I was soon to find out, though.

Sixteen and with a child. I was in no shape, no condition to be having a baby—living in cars, crashing on drunkards' couches, and making booze my top priority. My ONLY priority! So, I chose to terminate. I justified it by thinking the child would have been born with so many defects that it wasn't right.

I had no home and no way of raising a child. And worse, I knew I would never stop drinking. How could anyone bring someone into this world under those conditions? It wasn't fair. None of it was fair. I truly believed it was for the best. The truly saddening part is that I repeated this two more times.

I believed the lies of two separate individuals when they said, "I'm sterile, I can't have children," or "I love you and will never leave you."

Well, one had functioning sperm, and the other had left. I listened to the deceit and felt right at home with it. I am guilty of three deaths that still torment me. I have serious mixed emotions about my decisions. I realized I wasn't ready for any of those responsibilities. I couldn't even take care of myself. I make no excuses, but I will someday face the One who will judge me. Until then, I will pray for forgiveness.

CHAPTER 6

TRY TO BE GROWN-UP

I married for the first time at the age of 16. It was a sort of "guarantee" that I would never have to return to my mother's home. Of course, it wasn't legal, but Rowdy had "signed off" permission for it to take place. She must have thought "good riddance" as she wrote her name on the bottom of the simple piece of paper granting permission. My soon-to-be husband was eight years older than me, but it was better than the alternative of trying to live on my own or with Rowdy. It was my ticket out—my planned exit strategy from hell.

Then, I married again at the age of 19 to the person who became the father of my two children. At first, it was all fun and games—best friends getting drunk, driving around in his yellow and white Jimmy Blazer, climbing hills, and chasing the party scenes. Later on, we would attempt to "play house" and start a family, but that only interfered with our alcohol use. Sad but true. I honestly believe that if alcohol hadn't controlled our lives, we would have stood a chance. I also believe that the only good thing that came out of that failure was my kids.

My third marriage was never going to work because I completely lied to this man. It started with my intentions, which were not good to begin with. I needed to obtain my rights for my daughter, who was in the custody of the state, and I desperately wanted her back. The system had mentioned that "if I just had a stable home, it would be much easier." So that was the only answer—get a husband with a house. And I did exactly that.

After my daughter moved in with my new husband and me, I still wasn't ready to give in to motherhood. Pathetic but true. I continued my spiral downward—sneaking off to get high and pretending to be normal when I got back home. That lasted about ten months, and then he left. I can't blame him. And then my daughter left, too.

She went to live with her grandma again. I had already lost both of my children to the state once before due to my addictions. I realize now what a terrible nightmare all of it was—not just for me but especially for my children. I am so incredibly sorry to my children, "K" and "M." Deeply and sincerely apologetic.

I cannot say thank you enough to the lady (Grandma B) who cared for my children when I was a complete mess. She didn't have to, but she rescued them from their own mother. She never hesitated. Ever.

(Thank you, Grandma B.)

I honestly thought I could settle down and become "normal," to become the perfect little housewife with the perfect little family. I gave it a go—mostly, kinda, sorta. That lifestyle was never going to come to fruition because my desire to be numb was much greater than anything in this world. And it certainly didn't help that the men I chose needed "fixing," so I became obsessed with trying to save them, heal them, fix them, and turn them into men.

I thought I needed—or wanted them. And all that time, I should've been trying to save myself. From myself. Hmmm... I guess I saw my only worth in rescuing others. Sigh.

CHAPTER 7

KIDS

My biggest regret of all time is the fact that my children fell victim to my usage, even at their young ages. In my mind, I thought I was a decent mom, but I was *so* far from that honor. Yes, it *is* an honor to be a mother. I wish I would've learned that much earlier.

The house was clean, there was food in the cupboards, and they had decent clothing, but their mother was missing. The one person they were supposed to look up to and learn from. The one person they both needed. The one person they wanted was their mom. I would justify my poor parenting with statements like, "I did a better job than my mom!" Wow. But, in fact, I had become my own mother. I had become Rowdy.

I was nowhere to be found—always in the bars—and even if I was physically present, I'm sure mentally, I was not. I failed them. Repeatedly. Miserably. For years. And years. And years to come. I made so many mistakes, and then I would just add to them. How, you ask? By teaching them how to abuse the same drugs I was using. I led them down a path that *was* proven to be destructive and chaotic. I killed any possibility of their future.

I stole it and replaced it with "devil dust" (meth). I taught them how to steal, lie, use people, and become master manipulators. To get what they wanted by taking it. We were all best friends at one time... until we weren't. Eventually, my children and I would all be using those toxic chemicals together. Meth conquered the weak in us. It devoured us. It swallowed us. It destroyed us.

There are no excuses for what I did, and my regret runs deep. I destroyed my own children, and their lives were forever changed. I was no better than the person who gave birth to me, the one who ruined my life.

My apologies will never be enough, but to my two children, "K" and "M"—I am deeply and truly sorry for all you endured, learned, and suffered from. You both deserved so much more. I love you. My only hope is that after I am gone, I will leave you both with a better version of myself and with better memories. And I pray for true forgiveness, as I will always continue to seek it.

CHAPTER 8

WHAT WORK?

My employment history was very spotty and barely existed. I couldn't keep a job due to my raging addictions. Drugs took priority over everything. I would bounce from bartending (convenient, huh? At least I could get drunk on the job!) to waitressing to picking up an odd job here and there.

I even tried some more professional roles: administrative assistant at the BLM, photographer with my own studio space, or truck driver hauling ammonium nitrate. But when your hangover prevents you from going to work in the morning, they tend to let you go. Fired. Bye, bye.

Another reason for being jobless was the men in my life. They always had raging emotions of jealousy and accusations of betrayal. I was called a "whore" and constantly accused of "cheating"—completely unfounded, unwarranted, and most definitely undeserved.

Physical abuse was yet another reason I couldn't hold down a job. The recent beating from whatever man I was with at the time would leave me too embarrassed and humiliated to attend work. With a face mangled and covered in black, blue, and shades of purple, I didn't want anyone to know, and I didn't want to explain—have to lie to cover it. No amount of makeup could hide it. It was pointless. And so, so obvious.

I would pretend everything was well. Everything was normal. Let me tell you that takes great strength. I even attempted college for a while. I took registered nursing courses and made it almost two years. But I had strange feelings that something wasn't quite right—that something was missing. It just wasn't for me.

So, I gave up. I quit. Was it the pressures of home life? The drug life? Booze? Life itself, maybe? I didn't know. Just another failure to add to the many that already existed. So, I moved on to the next "adventure," not sure that's what I'd call it, but...

Anyway, I decided to try my hand at heavy equipment operation, and I absolutely fell in love with it. Getting greasy and dirty, with the smell of oil in the air, was my thing. I really enjoyed the course and even finished at the top of my class. By the end of the course, the professor had me doing some of the instructing—that's how good I got.

Eventually, I did some local work at a feed store, driving semi-trucks and hauling ammonium nitrate, delivering it to farmers' fields. But I quickly grew bored. I started bringing booze and my paraphernalia to work. I was getting drunk and/or high on the job—out in some farmer's field, out of my mind. That didn't last long, either. The job got in my way. So, I quit. Yet again.

Maybe my mom was right. I would never amount to anything, and I was a failure. I believed those words for a very long time.

CHAPTER 9

THE DARK MAN

After three failed marriages, two kids, and spiraling even further into the depths of hell, my drug usage became even more toxic. I met the "Dark Man," and he showed me how to escape reality. To really be numb, with no cares in the world. No more madness or sadness— just comfortably paralyzed. Outside my own self, I was erased.

My soul was depleted. My mind obliterated. Sticking needles in my arms and escaping was now my destiny. Syringes became my only true friend. My using was constant, from morning till night, but the night never ended. I remember being up for 18 days straight once. No sense of the real world outside.

During daylight hours, we "tweakers" usually stayed indoors (mainly because we didn't want anyone seeing us like that). Injecting meth into my arms (or wherever I could find a usable vein) became my daily passion. I lost weight. I lost my mind. I lost myself. It got so bad that I would shoot water into my veins when I had nothing else available. It was absolutely disgusting.

I continued using it intravenously for years. My veins are shattered and destroyed, thick scarred tissue now lying beneath my skin. They will never heal. A painful reminder of a disastrous lifestyle. I think the only reason I quit shooting up was because I couldn't "hit" myself anymore.

I had to ask someone to poke me with needles filled with a liquid that kills. It's truly a wonder that I'm still here. How did I not fall victim to overdose or "hot shots" (syringes filled with lethal substances with the intent to kill)? How did I not disappear like so many do? How was I not kidnapped when I wasn't coherent? Or raped? Or, worse yet... killed.

Why didn't I die? Why did I live? At that time, I probably would have welcomed death. Chances are likely.

CHAPTER 10
METH'D UP

Methamphetamines will divide a family quicker than anything and everything. It creates distance, doubt, and betrayal. It is a silent master and so devastatingly powerful. Lies become the truth, and the truth is never to be found. There is no way out. It feels hopeless—like being sucked into a vacuum and crudely disposed of. Chewed up, spit out, and destroyed. Helpless.

It shreds you from the inside out and then rips your face off while you watch. It stretches you from limb to limb and crushes your spirit. You will hit rock bottom, but scream for more. It eats your mind and robs you of your sanity. This is why it's called "devil dust."

Not only did I ruin my children's perspective on a good lifestyle, but I also sabotaged everything and everyone in my path for this drug. I dated dealers so I could get it for free. I stole for this drug. I robbed people and businesses of this drug. I did whatever I had to do to get my daily fix. I had so many different scams going that it was almost hard to keep up. I even gave myself away to get high, to get that drug. Horrid. Absolutely horrific.

We tweakers would hang out in "trap houses." The name comes from the sense of being trapped. Once you got inside, you were stuck there, with no escape. These places were usually rundown buildings, houses, or apartments, often without electricity or water. The stench of body odor, sex, and drugs filled the air with a strange metallic odor from meth being smoked.

Used needles lay in plain sight. Trap houses were filled with addicts just trying to feed their habits. These drug circles of mine only grew worse. Thieves, liars, and cheats, only out for themselves. No one is to be trusted. At one point, my own truck was stolen from my driveway! Chaos and drama ran rampant. No sense of reality. No sense of purpose. No sense of self-worth. No sense.

I became a master manipulator and almost always got what I wanted. The people I used had no idea they were being played. I read them like an open book and played them like a professional violinist. I worked them all well. I took and never gave back. Pathetic and sickening behavior. Saddening.

(If you are one of those people, I profoundly apologize.)

Meth makes you do things you never thought you were capable of. Things you would never, EVER do. Brain activity is seriously lacking—invisible. There are no real good highlights from this time in my life. Only wicked choices were made on my part. No good memories. Not that I would want to remember them anyway.

CHAPTER 11

A BLUR

My life was consumed by the wicked decisions I kept making over and over again. I found myself in and out of jail, one rehab facility, and several psychiatric hospitals. Suicide attempts had been my cry for help—overdosing on pills, slitting my wrists, and even putting my gun to my right temple and pulling the trigger. I'm still unsure why it didn't go off. It did every other time I used it. Hmmm... I was just so desperate for someone, for anyone, to show me kindness and love.

My attempts to end my life spanned years. I could never manage to subtract myself from this world. I wondered why I just couldn't get it right. My mind was filled with thoughts like, "I failed at that too!" and "I'm a real loser." I thought I would never amount to anything. I could hear Rowdy and her devastating words of unbelief echoing in my brain.

So, more bad men, and definitely more drugs and alcohol, were my future. More abuse and more dissolving of my soul—what was left of it, anyway. It was a vile lifestyle. I figured this was where I belonged. This was the path chosen for me. Or was it?

My 30s and 40s are pretty much a blur. A drug-using, alcoholic criminal—that's who I was. Breaking into homes and cars, stealing to survive or feed my habits, and doing so much wrong to others. I hurt people: assaulted, attacked, and even kidnapped the wrong people to collect for a drug debt.

The funny thing is, the debt wasn't even owed to me! But that was the deal I made to get some free drugs. Be a bully. A pit bull demanding payment. Then I would receive a reward, a baggie filled with a white, rocky substance: meth. How disturbing it is to think and act in such a moronic way.

That wasn't living. It was barely existing, barely surviving—just getting by. Trying to make it to and through another day. It's a slow death: progressive and aggressive. And eventually, it leads to criminal ways. Let me tell you about some of mine.

CHAPTER 12
CRIMINAL ACTIVITIES

There was one time, in my drugged-up state of mind, when I held someone at gunpoint! Only until he located the bike that I had loaned him (It wasn't even mine! I had stolen it from my ex!). Incredibly disturbing behavior, I know. Granted, the gun I was waving around was only a BB gun, but he didn't know that. I scared him terribly.

He was crying, pleading with me to remove the pistol from his face. I'm sure he had thoughts of dying an unexpected, unwelcomed death. No doubt it was a terrifying experience for him. It ended with him running for his life and hiding inside someone's home (I'm not even sure if he knew these people, but thankfully, they opened their doors). In all actuality, I'm so glad that he got away. I can only imagine the possibility of an awful outcome. Whew.

Later, I found myself in another predicament, another situation. Another drug-induced scenario. Another bad decision. Another bad time. Another bad man. Another bad reaction. Another, another, another. This time, I was facing 20 years in prison for running over a bad man, whom I will call "Jack." We were dating and, of course, doing drugs together. Same ol', same ol'.

Anyway, I had plowed him down with my ¾-ton truck. I drove right over the top of a human body—a real, live body. Despicable.

Let me take you back to how this started. A few months before the "runover" took place, I had taken a beating from Jack. It was so incredibly terrible that I literally looked like the "elephant woman" for weeks and weeks. My face was pulverized beyond recognition.

Upon picking him up from a drug den, the atmosphere was filled with rage and anger, and then violence soon broke out. He ripped the rearview mirror off my truck's window and began smashing it against my face. Over and over and over again. I remember counting six times as it continued to strike me.

When he wasn't satisfied with those results, he added his fists. His heavy punches landed on my cheeks, lips, nose, and eyes. I tried to escape, to slide out of the driver's seat, but my body was frozen with fear. I couldn't move—a state of shock and disbelief.

He jumped out and ran around to the front of the truck, tearing off the windshield wiper, only to attack me with it. Striking me repeatedly. I didn't count the lashings this time. My feet never touched the ground as he held me by my neck, trying to strangle me. All the while, he attempted to put my head through the truck's rear window with great hatred.

I knew I was dying. I couldn't breathe. I couldn't fight back. My body went limp, and my life was slipping away. Slow, agonizing death. Helpless and weakened. Powerless. Strange to think how I almost welcomed the loss of my own life. Maybe it was better this way?

And then, suddenly, as if an angel appeared, I heard the sound of a strange lady screaming at the top of her lungs, "STOP IT! YOU'RE GOING TO KILL HER!!!"

On the second story of this building stood a woman, doing her best to protect me, to save me from the hands of the devil. And I believe, without a doubt, that her words, her intervention, saved my life. I would have ceased to exist if not for her. (Thank you to MY angel.)

Several months after this horrific beating, I happened to be driving by the area where he lived. Seeking drugs was on my mind, of course. I was coming down, so I needed to come back up. I needed my daily intake, my "fix." Needed to get high. Needed. Strange word sometimes.

Anyway, Jack threw dirt clods or rocks at my truck, hitting the rear panel. Extreme fury filled my soul. Anger coursed through my veins with great ferocity! I spun that truck around, screeched the tires, jumped the sidewalk, and plowed him down. I ran him over with a ¾-ton truck!

Simply out of control! It really seemed so surreal (still does), like something straight out of a movie. But it was real. Very real. My mind blacked out most of it, and to this day, I can hardly recall all the details. Probably not necessary. Certainly disturbing. What I find very concerning is the thought that I wouldn't protect myself, but I would defend my vehicle. Wow. Pretty sad.

He survived. I am grateful for this. And I can only hope that he is living a better life now. (If you are reading this, my sincerest apologies for my actions. I wish you well.)

Another time, I was so desperate to get to the truth that I would do just about anything to find out what I already knew. I was aware that the man I was seeing at the time (I will call him "Mark") was cheating and lying to me.

I wasn't too concerned with the fact that he was sleeping with other people, but the fact that he was using drugs WITHOUT me. Hmm. I hated that part! I hated all the parts!

My one question was, "Why wasn't I good enough for him?"

I did everything I was told to do. I did everything he wanted me to do, no matter what. There were no limitations. None. I satisfied his every desire, or so I thought. I even did the really wicked stuff that I said I would never EVER do! I bowed down to him like he was a god. Like he was a king. I was his servant and his slave. I had to obey, always. My only goal was to please him. To have him love me. Why couldn't he just love me? And only me? What else did I have to do? The cost would become too much.

My quest to get to the truth turned into an obsession, and my actions roared with such ugliness. It was not my finest hour, and it was certainly not commendable by any means. But when you're high, you don't think like a normal person would. You think outside the box. There IS no box... 'Cause there's no rational thinking. AT ALL. PERIOD.

And then my meth mind took over. I held the truth in my very hands—the actual proof of his unfaithfulness, his lies, his deceit, his betrayal. But I needed him to say it.

I deserved the truth. So...

I would force him to tell me.

CHAPTER 13

BACKFIRED

In my basement was a chair with rope and duct tape nearby. My plan was to entice Mark downstairs and then coerce the truth out of him. "Coerce" is just another way of saying that, no matter what, I would force him to speak something other than lies. So, off to the dungeon for truth-telling time—just until he spoke with honesty.

Bad plan. Really stupid thinking. Thankfully, that never took place. But I will be honest: in the back of my messed-up mind, I really wanted it. What a way to find the truth.

Mark arrived at my place, and a violent argument soon erupted. Yelling, screaming, and many ugly curse words, all filled with rage. My son, who was living next door then, heard my pleas for help and came to my rescue. My body was being slammed against our adjoining wall, and that's when all hell broke loose!

As my legs dangled off the ground, Mark had his hands clenched tightly around my throat, cutting off any possible breath. I felt my life ending. This is how I would perish. My son, extremely enraged, protected his mother.

He shoved my abuser off me, and in doing so, Mark fell through the huge glass window, slicing open the main artery in one of his arms. Blood covered the entire front porch. The roof, the walls, the carpet, the tree outside, and even the grass in the front yard. There was blood everywhere. Everywhere.

He ran down the street and away from us, saving himself, with a bloody red trail following him. Adrenaline filled the air, along with disgust. Supposedly, he almost died from his injuries. Thankfully, he did not.

My plan had backfired most horrifically, and I was grateful that it had. Seeking the truth is never an easy thing to do, but I know now that you cannot go about it with evil and violence. It's wrong, and it cannot and will not be achieved.

Maybe the police knew the real backstory because no charges had been filed. Self-defense on my part. I will never know. It was just best to part ways.

CHAPTER 14

OUT OF CONTROL

After my terrifying experience with the law and the looming judgment of facing 20 years in prison, I went 'off the rails.' My addictions grew and grew, and I let them. I figured I was going away, so now was the time to really explode.

Get wild and crazy! Or at least crazier. Who would it hurt? And what did I have to lose? NOTHING. ABSOLUTELY NOTHING.

When I think back, I know I was trying to kill myself, maybe not in the 'traditional' ways, but by overdosing—either on alcohol or meth. I spent every day shooting up: in my arms, my legs, my neck, or even in my... butt. Yep, I said that. It's true.

Other users had told me about the GREAT benefits of this method. This was the way to go if you needed to reach that 'high' that seemed unattainable anymore. Literally, GO! My highs weren't numbing me any longer. I needed more and more and then some more. Bigger quantities, more in the baggie (and make sure it was nothing but rock—no powder. Guaranteed uncut, untouched). I lived for my addiction.

Needle marks ran up and down my arms. They became normal for me. Eventually, I could no longer 'hit' myself because of how much I had used. Scarred-up and thickened tissue prevented me from doing so. Now, I had to find other druggies to shoot me up. You'd think that would've been a sign to stop, but I didn't listen. Deep down, I just wanted to die.

Drink and drugs. Those were my goals. I just knew there had to be more to life than this. I had spent 50 years destroying myself. So, what now? Do I spend the next 50 years hating life? Hating the world? Hating people? Living with a heart full of hate?

No. It was time for a change.

CHAPTER 15

RUN AWAY

In May 2019, at the age of 50, I ran from the place that was keeping me sick. Not just from the town, but I ran from myself. I was the one who was keeping me sick. I became exhausted, so tired of using and abusing substances, of being used and abused, and just tired of the whole scene. I didn't want to hang out in drug dens anymore.

After my scare with prison, my thoughts of escaping became obsessive. I just couldn't do it anymore. That lifestyle wasn't working. That was NOT living. I don't even know if that was surviving. I felt like I was barely existing.

I desperately needed a new life. What did that entail? I had no idea whatsoever. I just knew there had to be something different, something better. Anything was better! I didn't want to suffer in turmoil for the next 50 years of my life. The first 50 were a complete disaster, so this change was crucial for me. But how? How do I change? What does it look like? Where do I go?

That's when I decided to do the exact opposite of everything I knew, of everything I had ever been taught or learned. I went to church. And everything changed.

CHAPTER 16

DOWN THE ROAD

During all this, I found one person who truly cared about me. My one and only dearest friend, Ross (who was/is not a drug user), helped me escape from my own demise. He had seen my struggles and only wanted me to do better, to succeed, to not die.

I don't think he was aware of my using meth, or maybe he was. He never said. He watched my downward spiral, and I am positive that is why he chose to help me, to save me from myself. (Thank you so much, and my deepest apologies for my lies and manipulation, Ross.)

There was no way for me to get out on my own. I had nothing—just a truck and a bunch of kitties. No money, no job. So, he was kind enough to loan me a fifth-wheel trailer to flee. He filled my truck with gasoline and even gave me money to leave.

And he kept on loving me from a distance. I don't blame him. I was toxic. So, I ran. Ran away. Free! Free!! Free!!! Or was I? I left with four cats, my ex-boyfriend, Mark, and several 'bindles' of meth. (A bindle is what addicts call their folded-up pieces of paper that contain their drugs.) Yep, I said that. I brought my nightmares with me.

Off to a great start! In the back of my mind, I knew this was NOT what I wanted. This is not who I wanted to be. I WANTED DIFFERENT. I NEEDED DIFFERENT! So, why was I messing it all up? Because I was terrified of being sober. I was terrified of doing the 'come down,' going through withdrawals, and sleeping for days at a time. I was terrified of not knowing who I would become. Would I like me? I feared reality.

But what now? My start was already a failure. What do I do? How do I end all of this? And then, God answered.

One morning, Mark had decided to get extremely intoxicated before 11:00! And I wanted nothing to do with it. That was the end! After I yelled at him to get sober, he bailed out. He jumped out of my truck and disappeared completely out of sight. I circled the blocks looking for him and finally returned to where my trailer had been parked. Later, he showed up so drunk that he had urinated all down the front of his pants. Wasted, and I was totally disgusted! No more. I'm done.

I phoned the police to have him removed from my bed, from my trailer. He was not going to pass out in my bed, not in his pee-pee pants! The police arrived and informed me that he had an outstanding warrant.

Mark had told me that the citation was issued because he failed to pay for services rendered at a convenience store years and years ago. That was not true. I discovered it was for sabotaging an old girlfriend's car. The officer stated that her 'brake lines had been cut.'

This was quite different from his side of the story. I trusted the officer.

God handled that situation, too. This is when I became single.

CHAPTER 17

SEARCHING

I spent the next year or so wandering, mostly circling where my daughter resided. (Oh, how I desperately wanted a relationship with her and my grandbabies!) Making the decision to visit churches wherever I went became my new purpose and goal.

Certainly, it couldn't hurt me. Could it? I did wonder if the church might burn to the ground or maybe I would be struck by lightning! How could a form of evil enter and not be extinguished? I was sure that nothing good could come of it, right? Wrong.

In all the churches I attended, I never felt judged or persecuted. These 'Jesus freaks' welcomed me with their arms wide open, big smiles on their faces and genuine love in their hearts. It didn't matter what church it was, whether in Washington State or Montana, no matter what city, I always encountered sincere and loving people. Strangers with love. Very odd, but fantastic altogether.

If only they knew who I was! I kept thinking. That didn't matter, though, because God knew. God knows. From the very start, inside my mother's womb, He created me to be His.

My journey to seek something better was weighing heavily on my heart and mind. And I knew I needed more. Finally, I was on my own.

CHAPTER 18

SEEKING

In 2020, the pandemic took over the world. Boy, did I ever feel alone! The whole world felt it. But it can be extremely trying when you're parked and living in an abandoned parking lot with no heat, electricity, water, family, friends, or anyone at all. My four kitties were stuck in isolation with an angry mom.

Living off the grid, sorta. Barely able to keep gas in my truck, but still able to buy beer. Drinking and drinking. Wake up and drink again. My body was feeling the impact. Vomiting became a daily routine, violently puking up booze and blood. Losing control of my bladder was normal. Vomit, beer, and pee: that was my odor. It's no wonder I soaked myself in body spray. Well, let me tell you something: YOU CAN'T COVER YOUR SHAME LIKE THAT. It doesn't work.

Because of this terrible time, my visits to the churches ceased. The only family I had was 55 miles away, so I kept trying to get closer to her, my daughter, and the town where she resided. Honestly, I just wanted to build a stronger, better relationship with her and be close to my grandchildren.

I bounced around a bit until I landed in an RV campground. At first, it wasn't so bad. It was more like hunting grounds for me, always on the prowl, looking for new drinking buddies. I found several and became a mooch, expecting others to fill my desire for alcohol.

I lived there for three years, and I felt myself deteriorating even more. I had no real friends; I was just stuck with myself, my own worst enemy. Drinking became all I wanted to do, which led to the destruction of any possible chance to reunite with my daughter. My behavior was unacceptable and erratic. She wanted nothing to do with me, and I could understand why. Once again, I wanted nothing to do with me.

I needed a new life. And I needed it soon! But how does someone like me start over? Is there a second chance? Yes.

CHAPTER 19

I KILLED HER

It was inevitable that a death had to take place. A murder was in order, and it was time for me to kill. Yes, I said kill. To kill me. The killing of Terri. She must die. I could no longer associate with 'her' and her disastrous ways. She had to go. And so... Terese was reborn. Terese is born. The name change had to take place.

Terri no longer exists and never will again. She is gone. Gone for good. No turning back. Good riddance! If I am to start over, I need to return to the name by which God knows me. The name given to me is Terese Mon Reve. Only then can I truly begin to grow.

So, after 47 years, I quit drinking. November 7, 2022, is my sober date. My body was literally shutting down, and I knew it was time. It was time to rescue me. Feelings of something better were 'calling' me to do something different. I can't explain it, but I just felt like there was so much more I was supposed to do. And the drinking was only detouring me, derailing me, sabotaging me.

Never in a million years would I have thought that a world without alcohol was possible, and I certainly could not see myself as a sober person. But I found the way out! As I write this story of mine, it is still hard for me to believe that this world exists. A sober world. Out of 55 years of my life, too many years were wasted by being wasted. Saddening. And very gross.

I struggled with trying to be a sober person every single day. My answer to every problem I had was gone. No idea how to truly live without my booze. My mind was consumed and confused. My body reacted with great hostility. I violently threw up, had headaches and shakes, couldn't eat, and couldn't sleep. But all in all, the worst part was that my cravings took over my brain.

So, I prayed. And I prayed. And I prayed even more.

"Please, God, help me through this. I can't live like this anymore! Please, Father. Please, please, help me."

And He did. I asked, and He answered.

The hours turned into days, then became a week, and then a couple of weeks, which, in turn, became months. As of March 7, 2024, I have 16 months of sobriety! No alcohol whatsoever! I am becoming sober! Becoming who I was meant to be. This journey is not an easy one, and relapses do happen. I am still only human. That's why I will not lie to you. That is not the goal of this testimony.

I did relapse, but not on booze on meth. It was while I was living at that campground (I swear that place was pure evil) back in 2022 when the devil showed me a baggie and a glass pipe, and I jumped on it. Shameful. No more excuses to use. It wasn't the campground; it was me listening to the devil's lies. It is so difficult to break those habits, that addiction, but I wasn't going to give myself permission to stay in my 'comfort zone of misery.'

There's that saying, "Once an addict, always an addict," right?

No! You don't have to live by that saying. You do not have to live up to that title. You don't have to be that person. You don't have to be drunk or drugged up. You don't have to be depressed or disgusted with life. You don't have to be drained or down and out. You don't have to accept defeat. It's not who you are. You CAN be different. You CAN be changed. You CAN be better. You CAN be loved. You CAN. Yes... YOU! You ARE worthy! And Father God is waiting for you. My sobriety is now to the point where I don't even really think about it. I am losing count of how many days, weeks, or months have passed. It's getting easier, day by day. It no longer has its sickening control over me. No more obsessing over it.

Don't get me wrong. I'm not saying that I don't have urges because I do. But it's usually after I struggle with something I can't control or when I am having a difficult day or time. The truth is that I know if I 'use', the road will lead me to certain death. I refuse to do the devil's work for him. I will not bring him back in by choosing drugs or alcohol.

I will continue to 'kick him out,' even if I must complete it with an 'opening of the door' and gesturing with a swift kick, exclaiming, "SUCK IT, satan! Not today! Or any day!"

I am choosing life. My road to recovery and finding Jesus is not an easy one by far. But it most definitely is the life I was chosen for. I have no doubts. At all. There is a reason for my existence. And if you are reading this, there is a reason for your being, too.

I spoke of having a 'feeling' earlier that I just knew I was meant for so much more. During these last two years, I became a 'regular' at church. In the beginning, I would show up (if I wasn't hungover) and sit in the far back, trying not to be visible, I guess.

My attendance was certainly lacking. But something about that place just kept drawing me back in. It was as if the Pastor was speaking directly to me as if the message was intended for me to hear. It tugged at my heart and made my mind reel with such curiosity.

I had questions that needed to be answered. I had feelings that were stirred up—but in such a good way. An overwhelming desire to be 'changed,' to be 'different.' I wanted what I saw in others: a calmness and a love that came from within. I craved this. I wanted more, so I chased after it.

CHAPTER 20

NEW LIFE

On November 20, 2022, I gave my life to the Lord. I was baptized in my home church in Polson, Montana. New Life Church gave me my new life. The reason I chose this place is its name. A new life is exactly what I was seeking.

That Sunday morning brought about the best decision I have ever made. I ran from the second-story balcony of the church and quickly proceeded down to the holding tank, where His living water was inside. Because of this quick decision, I was unprepared and had to improvise.

One of the 'leaders' adorned me with a t-shirt, and I wore my long-john winter fleece pants. I choose to be born again, to give myself to the Lord. Asked for forgiveness, and I repented. I was to become the daughter of the highest, the King of Kings, and the Lord of Lords, God. I am choosing to follow Him ALL the days for the rest of my life!

Suddenly, I was submerged into and under His Holy water, and when I arose from it, I was soaked to the bone BUT ALIVE for the first time. My body was covered in goosebumps, the blood in my veins became EXCITED, my heart was filled with fluffiness (best way to describe it!), and I could barely breathe. And I was filled with so much love!

My first words were, "I love you all!"

It was, and IS, the MOST INCREDIBLE feeling in all this world. I belong to God now. And ALWAYS will. I turned back to Our Father, and I became adopted. Baptized with the blood of Jesus Christ and made whole! He is mine, and I am His.

I am a daughter of a King. I am royalty. I am chosen and redeemed. Redeemed like a coupon; turn in your ticket for a better prize! That's ME! A valuable prize. A treasure. Precious to my Father. All my sins are forgiven. Not just some, but ALL of them! I am changed. I am different.

I am no longer promiscuous or a criminal. I am no longer an alcoholic or drug addict. I am no longer a manipulator or an abuser. I wear none of those titles. I went from vulgar swearing and using curse words obnoxiously to watching my mouth and speaking kind words of encouragement to others. I think before I speak. I always try my best to speak with words from God. I have learned that the tongue is a very powerful thing and can damage so easily. So, use it wisely.

I was obsessed with knowing more about my God and who Jesus really is! About the true love given to us. Selflessly. By a Father who loved me through all my sins, wickedness, and transgressions. Learning of REAL love. God's love. IT IS SOOOO REAL. It is a relationship that is indescribable and so pure. And it is available to ALL. YES, I said ALL!

Okay, now I sound like I am preaching. Well, I kinda am. Anyways…

Life isn't perfect, by any means, but just so you know, my life is **NOTHING** like before, If you haven't already figured that out. It is not filled with chaos and torment. No destruction or devastation. It's disgusting and pathetic. NO! Not even close. Far from it.

I know I have someone to go to when I face trials and tribulations. I run to my Father God. I do have my ups and downs, just like any other human being, and I'm not claiming to be perfect by any means. My aim is not for perfection. It is for peace. My life now is completely different. I am changed. I am a child of God.

I now get to experience so much love and kindness, whether I am giving it or receiving it. A generosity flows from so many hearts, and it completely surrounds me. A peace inside that is truly unexplainable and greatly welcomed! I have hope for a better tomorrow, and I know that my Father God has provided and will always provide for me.

He has prepared a place in Heaven for me. If you don't believe this is possible and could happen to you, I challenge you to try it. What do you have to lose? Are you tired? Are you tired of being tired? Are you sick? Do you struggle with addiction? Are you brokenhearted? Are you hopeless? Have you given up? **_DON'T!_** There is another way.

My suggestion is to go to a local church. Do it 3xs. I know that you will hear a message from someone who will reach into your very core. Your heart WILL be 'tugged' at through the words of a Pastor or a person attending, or maybe even a song.

God is there waiting for you.

CHAPTER 21

I'M TELLING

Then, God gave me an idea. I am His servant, and I am very eager to do whatever He is calling me to do. Invitations. He planted the seed of making up 'fliers' (I called them invites) and walking through the three cities that I currently live by.

The invites asked, "Feeling lost? Broken? Hopeless? Here is an invitation to your new life ..." at New Life Church.

My church sister, Pam, was kind enough to print out over 800 of them, and I walked from place to place as the winds blew and the snow fell. After all, it was during the months of March and April in Montana.

I called it my 'March it Out for the Lord' and 'April, His Will' adventure. It's called evangelism, and it is about sharing the good news about Jesus. Spreading the Good Word. I am ready to tell!

Some people have asked, "Why do you seek God after all He put you through?"

The answer to that is He didn't. He didn't put me through anything. I did. As a matter of fact, He is the one who pulled me through ALL OF IT. It wasn't some sort of test. Jesus was and is the reason why I am still here. He held out His hand, grabbed me by my right hand, and walked by my side, never leaving me.

For example, that waterfall, *MY WATERFALL,* my safe place, a vision of somewhere better to travel,   that's where God was waiting for me. Letting me see a slight version of Heaven and allowing me to escape from hell. The devil may have had his hands on me, but God took me from him. Time and time again. The depths of hell couldn't hold me.

Directly after my journey with my invites, my Pastor approached me and asked if I would be interested in sharing my story, to give my testimony. I was kinda in shock that anyone would want to hear about me. But that is what this is all about. I need to reveal, to heal. And my real hope is that my story will guide someone who is lost. To let them know, YOU ARE NOT ALONE. And there is hope! There is another side to your story.

So, I rehearsed what I would say at that stage for days. Terrified because I feared messing up, saying something wrong, tripping, stumbling, stuttering, fainting, and all that scary stuff. I have never done anything like that in my entire life, and not while being sober! YIKES!

When it was time, I couldn't believe the confidence I felt deep inside. My fears disappeared, and I spoke with intention and truth. No one judged me or shamed me. I saw faces that truly cared. I witnessed compassion and felt it at my very core. Love is what I saw and what I felt. Deep, sincere love. From people, I barely even knew. How strangely beautiful. Peaceful. And it was all mine.

I have gained so much after this amazing experience. I have a church family consisting of all sorts of brothers and sisters, and I even have a mom. A brand-new mom. In the hallway of our church, a woman, in all her elegance, came up to me. She introduced herself and spoke words out of love. And then 'adopted' me on the spot.

She said that since I didn't have much of a mother, she would be mine. I call her Momma J. She's kind, loving, generous, patient, intelligent, attentive... sober. She has truly been an inspiration and shares her great wisdom with me. She has this sense of calmness about her and an undeniable beauty. Au natural! God loves her deeply, and she shines Jesus. She is truly amazing, and I am so blessed to have her in my life. Thank you, Momma J.

I sure do love you!

CHAPTER 22

PERFECTLY LOVED

Around the same time, I was introduced to my sweet friend and sister in Christ, Deb. This wonderful woman accepted me into her life without hesitation and genuinely showed me kindness and a friendship never experienced before. She truly knows what being a friend means and how to serve the Lord.

Her teachings are always easy for me to digest, and she never gives up on me. Our relationship developed when we both attended a gathering for women, a retreat. There is a place up the road that hosts many different functions, but mainly lessons about loving God and pursuing a relationship with Him.

It is a Bible camp for men, women, and families, and it is drenched with the Holy Spirit and God's presence! LITERALLY! This one retreat, in particular, was only for women, and it was titled 'Perfectly Loved,' and it was AMAZING!

My new sister, Deb, and I drove up on a Friday and came back on Sunday. This was our first real get-together, and I must say that I was terrified! We had met up once before for coffee, but never an adventure with one another. My fears overwhelmed me. What if I said something wrong? Something stupid? Or what if I slipped and said a curse word? Or what if I don't understand it or get It?

The answer to all these questions is FEAR ONLY GOD. Simple. These worries were silly. Ms. Deb guided me through the whole weekend, and what came about was magnificent. I now have a very loyal and trustworthy friend and sister for life! She has been there for so much, and I honestly believe that she will be there till the end... and then some.

She has shown me her love over and over again. I will give an example. It's the one that means the most, the one that first comes into my mind when I think of her kindness. It was the time when I had to endure July 4 fireworks. I had been avoiding these loud explosions for years and years and years (with my severe PTSD, the situation became unbearable), but my sister Deb came to my rescue.

As I was crying, shaking, trembling, couldn't breathe, and trying to hide, there she was. She texted me with comforting words and suggested breathing and relaxation techniques while going through the same thing as I did. She suffers from the same condition. She was so strong and wise (and still is!), and I tried desperately to cope, but to no avail.

She realized my situation was not improving and came running. Ms. Deb showed up at my doorstep with a bag full of magical items (pens, papers, 'busy' stuff) and even a portable stereo to drown out the outside noises. Who does that? My sister Deb.

I am fighting back tears as I write this because I know that she truly loves me. She is never selfish and never asks for anything in return. She is always so glad to help and answer my silly questions. She takes the time for me and never passes judgment. Only genuine words of encouragement come from her mouth.

Her heart is pure, and her smile is powerful. She is real, and her love is too. She teaches me daily how to be a better friend, sister, and daughter of God. She reminds me of who I am, of who I am becoming, and the rewards we will both treasure someday. She is thoughtful and compassionate.

She brightens my every day and presents me with a cup of coffee on Sunday mornings, with the label 'Beautiful Terese' written in her own handwriting (she faithfully serves God by running this coffee cart for years and years, and more years... without a single complaint). She teaches me how to be a better friend and love people sincerely. She sees the positive in everything, even when she is in her agonizing pain.

She shows me how to listen to God and believe in who I truly am. She points out my achievements and marvels at my growth. She loves me perfectly. There is not a day that we do not communicate, a day without some good advice and a good lesson to be learned, or a day without overcoming the world. We have since found out exactly how alike we truly are.

Twins from different mommas, but we have the same Father. His name is God. She loves Him like I do. He is OUR reason. I can't imagine living this life without her and cannot wait to dance in Heaven with her. Pain-free.

I know that we will endure this world's trials together, so fear not. And I also know that we will conquer these tribulations with the help of our powerful Father. Our journey is far from over, and I look forward to growing up with you!

I love you, my dear, sweet friend and precious sister, till the end (and then some!). THANK YOU FOR IT ALL! I will always be here for you.

(If you ever decide to attend New Life Church in Polson, Montana, just look in the front row. That's where you'll find us! We sing loud! We cry often! And we dance to the beat of Jesus!)

BIG SHOUT OUT to Ms. Pam! Thank you for putting us together! You did SO GOOD! GRATEFUL

We both are.

CHAPTER 23

SOLID GROUND

Let me tell you how good God is...

My time had come to an end at the campground where I was living. Rent was due, and I had no more to give. Broke, with no place to go. I knew what needed to be done, so I got on my hands and knees, and I **PRAYED**. I prayed for an answer. I prayed for a place that would accept me. I prayed for someone to give me a chance. I prayed. And I prayed.

AND WITHIN 3 DAYS' TIME, GOD ANSWERED!

He gave me my Pops, Mike Lee, and his beautiful wife, Sharon. This incredible couple would change my life in even greater ways. They would fill my life with a love that I had NEVER known existed. THANK YOU BOTH!

Feelings of anxiety and fear filled me as I moved my fifth-wheel trailer into the backyard of a total stranger. Granted, he was a fellow member of my church, but I had not met him until this day of June 2, 2023.

An older man with a huge smile appeared from the doorway of his big, two-toned white and brown mechanical shop to help me position my home. He introduced himself as Mike, eager to help me, but I refused.

After so many years of doing things on my own, it was very difficult for me to accept anything from anyone. My silly thoughts would be, *What do they REALLY want? There had to be a reason behind the generosity. It couldn't just be a nice gesture. A genuine kindness. Could it?*

YES, IT COULD.

The backyard was filled with junk cars and oil stains on the grounds. Once again, my fears ran rapidly. I dreaded possible injuries for my kitties and maybe even death. I truly believed that I had made a huge mistake.

BOY, WAS I EVER WRONG! BIG TIME.

There was and is a very strong presence that saturates this place. A feeling of holiness. Of goodness. A real sense of peace. I soon realized that this was no mistake. This was all part of God's plan. He lives here. And this is where He wants me.

So, I started building. I began with a yard.

CHAPTER 24

BLOSSOM

Soon after moving in, I created my very own paradise. I began by raking rocks to plant grass seeds. My intentions were to cover up most of the oil slicks outside my door. Make something beautiful. The first attempts didn't 'take,' so I tried and tried again.

Slowly, it grew thicker in some places and not so thick in others. It was perfect! Later, I would add some potted flowers, along with a fern, which needed lots of loving tender care. She (my fern) came into full bloom and really looks great now. God did most of the work. I just added the water.

He always does most of the work. Thank You, Father God. Anyway, I felt myself slowly coming out of my shell. I was starting to learn that I was safe here, which was NOT easy for me to do. AT ALL.

I had to realize that this lil' ole man was not here to hurt me, but to help me. He had already responded by letting me reside on his property. He plugged me into his electricity and even supplied me with water.

He offered me access to his shop and bathroom facilities. What else did I need for proof? That is HUGE! There was not one thing that this kind man held back from me. His generosity exploded from his very being, and I could feel my heart gradually accepting him.

He became my Pops! My Pops-A-Doodle. My Pops granted freedom, security, and safety. I was given the opportunity to really BLOSSOM. TO GROW. I want to strengthen not only myself but also my relationship with my Father, God. This is the perfect place to do that. To find out more about Jesus and His ways. I see so many brothers and sisters in the church that I just wanted what they all have. I wanted it for myself. I craved it, and it became my obsession. Literally!

And on this Holy Ground, this magical chunk of land that God placed me on, was the ideal place to dive into MORE. God had planted a seed. And that seed was ME.

CHAPTER 25

DADDY DAUGHTER TIME

It began with a step up, literally. He provided me with a blue plastic pallet to help me get into my trailer more easily. My stairs were a little far from the ground, but they're not anymore! How kind and very thoughtful. Then, he stabilized my trailer. This rickety ol' trailer (1991 version) was swaying from side to side, so Pops came up with an idea. And let me tell you that when he says, "I got an idea!" it's ALWAYS a good one, and it ALWAYS works! He is so smart! Love his wisdom.

Anyway, he came up with a way to prevent it from moving any longer. It sits SOLID now. First time in 5 years for that to happen. I can jump inside, and everything stays in place. Thank you, Pops.

He built a roof so the rain and snow don't seep into the carpets inside. What a nice feeling that is. Stays dry now. Crazy. No more carpet removal or mold growing. The yucky smell of mildew has even disappeared. Thank you, Pops.

He gave me a bench to work on my many different projects, but I have rarely used it, so it has basically become a storage shelf! Oops. He gave me a place to hang my clothes, which have always been taking up residence in my bathroom shower, preventing me from ever being able to use it until now! That is a SENSATIONAL feeling. I can be washed clean in my own home. WOW. Thank you, Pops.

Before that, he built a stand for my homemade tub. It is a watering trough for animals, usually for cows and horses, but it works fantastic! I had it outside at first, and then winter hit. So, he let me bring it into his shop. Providing me with heat and comfort inside.

This remarkable man has done so much for me that it's almost hard to remember. The little things are nothing to him. He doesn't really make a fuss over anything. I believe that he truly just loves to be useful and helpful. And he does an excellent job at both!

He fixed an antenna so I could have two TV channels, made a flower hanger for my fern outside, and helped me adjust my awning repeatedly. Taped up my windows so the cold wouldn't come in anymore and gave me heaters so I could make it thru these cold Montana winters. Repaired so many extension cords that I somehow kept burning up. This man has SO MANY talents. He is unbelievably capable.

He has taken care of me while I was sick and even drove me to the hospital and stayed by my side, never leaving. That has NEVER EVER happened in my life. I cry just thinking of this. He held my hand just like a dad would do and comforted me in such an amazing way. I liked it. A lot! Even after my shoulder surgery, he was there. With no complaints, he just cared. Such a strange and wonderful feeling. Is this what it's like to be loved? YES is the answer.

He checked on me regularly and brought me bags of ice for the swelling. He picked up my meds and made sure I was tucked in and not tangled in my cords. Tears fill my eyes when I think of how truly beautiful this man is!

He has fixed SO MUCH stuff on this trailer that I don't even know where to begin! The front door now closes, and the screen hinges no longer gouge out my arms as I walk through. It even locks properly now! Whoa, what a concept. The water no longer leaks outside, and the pressure is top-notch.

The propane heat batteries work like they are supposed to now because he came up with a better solution to that problem. This smart man added a much more efficient battery charger than I had, and it works. Thank you, Pops.

The list goes on. At 74 years young, this man is unstoppable! My truck was our next adventure. We started by replacing the taillights and a missing door handle, then moved on to the seriously damaged tailgate. I wanted it gone. Too many bad memories.

The company I ordered my tailgate from kept sending a damaged product (they sent it twice. It was very frustrating), so Pops decided to just fix it, to remove all the dents and bends in the steel. This man really knows what he is doing! Professionally skilled. And then, he scuffed it all down and painted it white, matching the original color perfectly. He also buffed it! And it IS MAGNIFICENT!

The old is out, and the new has begun. He welded the exhaust system into which I had drilled holes. (This is a very long story... and perhaps I will share it sometime). He replaced my oxygen sensors and ran codes on my truck (to establish what was wrong with it).

He gave me a trick on how to clean up my headlights (WD40!) and helped me get the seat covers on. Also, showed me how to get my back seat down after 13 years of owning this vehicle! WOW. There is truly NOTHING that this generous and beautiful being would not do for me. NOTHING.

If I mention something needs fixing or I have an idea of some sort, it seems like he uses those times as an opportunity for him to be useful. Maybe at the age of 74, it gets kinda boring, or possibly running out of projects or things to do? I would imagine that a lot has been accomplished by then.

My desire to build fires outside did not go unnoticed. I really enjoy watching the night skies and listening to the sounds of the crackling wood (that he also provided and even chopped up for me), so he constructed a firepit out of an old transmission case, and it works phenomenally well! Like I said, it is ALWAYS GOOD when he has an idea.

My Pops has gone way beyond what I could have ever expected. He became the dad that I never had. I cannot explain how truly wonderful this man is. He has taken over my heart and filled that void I have been carrying for so long. I love him. Dearly. TRULY.

My wants and needs are always taken care of. When my kitty needed a vet, Pops jumped in to help, never questioning me one bit. If I need toilet paper, dish soap, or gas in my truck, he does not hesitate. He is there every morning when I need a hug, waiting for me with open arms. He blesses me with his very presence daily.

Dinner invites are a regular thing now, and I absolutely love it. My childhood had never experienced family dinners, that's for sure. It was a 'fend for yourself' situation. And I must say, my Pops is an excellent chef, so I attend as much as possible. Plumping me up, he is! And I'm okay with that.

It sure does melt my heart. His love for me is unbelievable. His kindness and patience are so admirable. He has accepted me with all my flaws and imperfections and even accepted me with all my cats (7ish... 6 of my own and one stray). Most people would have hesitated, but he did not. He is an exceptional human being and so deserves all the things that he desires.

The wisdom that he displays is incredible, truly beyond this world. His patience and lack of anger teaches me who I want to become. The kindness and sincerity he showers me with are genuine, freely given to me, and very welcomed.

My Pops treats me like I am one of his own. No need for a birth certificate or adoption papers. I found a family. A family that loves me. I am a daughter of a GOOD MAN, of a GREAT MAN. He makes me feel like I am wanted and that I belong. Like I am not garbage, and I am valuable. Worthy of love and of being loved.

These feelings are above anything I could have ever imagined. I owe this to you, my Pops. You have changed my world, and I will never be the same, and it's because of you. You are the reason for this book. Your encouragement is all I needed. You are my Dad.

Thank you for being my mentor. I really do look up to you. Thank you, Pops. I sure do love you!!!

CHAPTER 26

FATHER TIME

Every day became a search for more.

My mornings start (present tense, still actively doing this routine) out with a grateful heart by saying, "Thank You, Father, for letting me wake up."

I realize there are a lot of people who don't get the chance, and it truly saddens my heart. So, I show gratitude. Then, of course, comes the Armor of God. I ask my Father God for His protection. I ask Him to cover my family, friends, loved ones, myself, and even my kitties (YES, I am a little strange, and that is okay!)

Here's how I ask...

Father God,

I ask that You equip my feet so that they are ready to spread the Gospel of peace. I ask that You put on the belt of truth and buckle it around my waist. Place the breastplate of righteousness in its place. Put on the helmet of salvation, which keeps out ALL evil thoughts and words. Then, my sword of the spirit, which is the Word of God.

Finally, my shield of faith, which extinguishes ALL the fiery darts of the evil one.

AMEN

Lastly, I will follow up with the Lord's Prayer. You know the one,

Our Father, who art in Heaven. Hallow be thy name.

Thy Kingdom come, thy will be done, on Earth as it is in Heaven.

Give us this day, our daily bread, and forgive us our trespasses, as we forgive those who trespass against us.

And lead us NOT into temptation but deliver us from evil.

For thine is the Kingdom, and the power, and the glory,

FOREVER

and ever and ever

In Jesus' name

AMEN.

This prayer was hard for me to understand at first, so I am going to do my best to decipher it for you, breaking it down. Expect lots of parentheses.

* **Our Father** (God, who is your ONLY Father. Earthly men are labeled dad, Papa, Pops, but never Father. There is only one Father, and that is God)

* **Who art in Heaven** (art = lives, dwells)

* **Hallow be thy name** (hallow= Holy)

* **Thy Kingdom come** (Heaven is ours)

* **Thy will be done** (His will is for us to LOVE)

* **On Earth as it is in Heaven** (Heaven is HIS perfect design)

* **Give us this day, our daily bread** (this is NOT actual food. This is referring to the Bible, our 'manual' for living a good and righteous life. Read it! Daily.)

* **And forgive us our trespasses** (forgive our sins)

* As we forgive those who trespass against us (forgive others for their sins. Very important! If God forgives us, then how can we not do as He asks us to?)

* And lead us not into temptation (this is everything NOT of God., for example, adultery, lying, stealing, lust, gluttony, greed, wrath, envy, and pride.)

* But deliver us from evil (keep us from the wicked one and his schemes. I am speaking of satan, the devil)

* For thine is the Kingdom, the Power, and the Glory (thine means 'Yours' as in God... so HIS Kingdom is Heaven. It holds the power and all the glory to come!)

* Forever and ever (pretty self-explanatory)

* AMEN (which means, 'SO BE IT'.. in agreement)

Hope that helps!

All of this is done before I even pull back my covers on my bed. I will NOT stop doing this because I honestly believe if I am 'PRAYED UP' for the day, I stand a better chance at the ways of this world. YES AND AMEN. YES AND AMEN!

After I am done with these prayers, I pour a cup of coffee and surrender myself to my journal and my devotionals (approximately 7). My journaling consists of 3 sections. The first is I jot down a song lyric that is placed in my head (I know this is the Holy Spirit and HIS song to me, every single morning! Different songs daily).

Then, I write about the previous day and all the good stuff (and icky) that happened. Lastly, I give thanks to the Lord. Being grateful is key! On the bottom are seven hearts, symbolizing my love for God. I have filled up many, many journals.

The devotionals contain many scriptures and follow the Bible accurately. One of my favorites is called 'Jesus Calling' by Sarah Young or even 'Our Daily Bread,' which is free. These devotionals guide me and educate me each and every single day. I have been doing this faithfully for almost two years and can't even imagine my days without these practices.

I highly recommend everyone try it or something like it. Why not start your day by being grateful, getting armored up, and talking to God? What does it hurt? It just might help!

I attend a Bible study on Tuesday evenings with some of God's wonderful children. I am one of the youngest members, and I am grateful for all the knowledge they are willing to share. Learning so many incredible things always piques my curiosity, which leads to more questions. Superb lessons. The mysteries of God. Continues and continues! I am in awe. Good job, God! You really DO know what you're doing! Duh

I ask for blessings on ALL my food, even if it is a small cookie. It comes from God, so I need to ask for HIS blessings and show gratitude. Be thankful. I pray for others on a regular basis. Whether it's an ambulance wailing its sirens or a life flight helicopter rushing to the nearest hospital. I could only hope that if I was in that position, that someone would be kind enough to pray for me. I show genuine care for God's people.

I even thank the crosses on the side of the highways by saying, "Thank you for being an Angel."

It's obviously a tragic scenario, and I guess I just need them to be recognized. Silly? Maybe. Not to me, though.

I would also like to mention a great radio station (also a FREE app for your phone) that I listen to quite regularly. It is called 'KLOVE'.

It is Christian-based, and the songs they play are always uplifting and inspiring. This radio station is broadcast throughout the States, and I promise you it will change you. There is no way anyone can walk away without feeling uplifted and grateful. Take the 30-day challenge (of listening) to see what happens next!

At night, I do my nightly ritual of reading a prayer from a Bible app on my phone. Followed by faithfully reading my *actual* Bible. The Bible is the way to learn how to live a righteous life. It is an 'instructional manual' on how to do so. It is God's word, which is truth. It is a love letter from Our Father God. It never fails to amaze me that if I need something answered because my curiosity has taken over, I will always find what I am seeking. It's ALL in there!

Strangely enough, it appears that God directs me towards certain scriptures for that day's lessons. That is odd but true. I feel like I am right where I am supposed to be, and I receive confirmation, constantly acknowledging my progress.

I am building a beautiful relationship with God. It grows stronger every day, and I am starting to realize that He will NEVER leave me and will always provide for me. ALWAYS! NO MATTER WHAT! Sometimes, I forget (I am still quite new to all of this), but I do know that He makes a way when there is none. Even when I can't see it, He does.

All are part of His plan. His way is SOOOO much better than mine. Because of my human qualities, I tend to mess things up. So, I lean into Him.

His will is my will.

So, here comes the preachy part.

How do you go about this change?

1. **Find a church** and attend it regularly.

2. **Get baptized**. Give your life to the Lord.

3. **Read your Bible**. Every day!

And BELIEVE.

Then, stand back and watch Him work.

How do you erase all the bad stuff you have done?

REPENT AND BE BAPTIZED.

BELIEVE

AND

RECEIVE

CHAPTER 27

CRASH COURSE

So, I remember when I first got started on this journey and how confused I was when people would speak of God, or Jesus, or the Holy Spirit. They are 3 in 1. The Trinity. God is the creator of ALL. That means He is the one who created you and me and the skies and seas. Jesus is His son, who was tortured and beaten and died on the cross For ALL of us. For our sins. The Holy Spirit is what Jesus left us ALL with. An invisible instructor of sorts. This spirit lives in us and guides us.

There are 2 'sections' of the Bible.

* The Old Testament is all about God and His people and the foretelling of the future. Of what was to come. It is very accurate.

* The New Testament is the coming of Jesus, of how He came to save God's children, US. He came for the brokenhearted and crushed in spirit. Once again, that is US.

There are many different 'versions' of the Bible, and if you are looking for an easy read, then I highly suggest the NIV (New International Version). The Bible is the same no matter what language it is in, and it will never change, just like Our Father God. He is a CONSTANT in our lives. He will NEVER change. He is the same God from thousands and thousands of years ago and wants us to come into HIS family.

Personally, I started with the New Testament. I NEEDED to know more about this guy named Jesus. Why would he die for me? For us? And how could He love people so easily? *Especially* the ones labeled 'shameful,' 'undesired,' 'unwanted,' or 'outcasts.' That was Me.

The Book of Matthew is a great beginning. I got hooked, and I haven't stopped yet. I never intend to. It's my new obsession. It's intriguing and extremely relatable to today's times.

The Bible is based on TRUTH from many, MANY witnesses.

And it predicts what is to come. ACCURATELY.

CHAPTER 28

IF YOU'RE WONDERING

I did find my mom's cat, Tiger. She came crawling back the next day unscathed. Since then, I have had my fair share of kitties. I guess you could call me a 'cat collector' of some sort. I simply cannot say no. I love them like God loves me. Unconditionally. And if you happen to know me, this is NOT an invitation for me to adopt anymore. I appreciate it, but I have plenty for now.

Recently, I learned how to forgive my mother. It is a very freeing feeling. I froze in front of my bedroom mirror, and I could see her face as I felt her presence. At that very moment, I was overwhelmed with sensations of sadness and empathy. I felt her struggles as a mother, as a person, and as an alcoholic.

Tears rushed down my cheeks, sobbing out of control, and then a radical madness of love flowed in. I forgave her. And I meant it. I must say that I have a much better relationship with her now, even if she is in Heaven. I talk to her all the time, and I know she hears me. I feel like she is reaching out to me sometimes. I hear things and see things that are a definite sign that she is with me.

It's true. I am still learning how to forgive myself. It's a daily process that I am continuing to journey on. I am on solid ground now, and there is no more quicksand. I still live in a borrowed fifth wheel, and I am learning to be content with what the Lord is providing me. I don't have much, but I have all I need. Besides, it's not what you have but what you can give. Love is free.

I live a rich life. Not monetarily by any means, but I have everything I need, thanks to my Father God. I want nothing at all. TRULY. I am rich in love.

Content.

I am happier, more at peace, and I love life for the first time ever. I am comfortable in my own skin, and it shows. I am giving, helpful, and kind at all times. I am genuinely changed in every way. I no longer wake up with hangovers and regrets. This is a brand-new world entirely! The lessons I was never taught, well, I am learning them now. Childhood teachings for a 55-year-old woman, and I am eager!

I am seeking God's wisdom, His kindness, and His patience, and I get to experience His *real* love DAILY. I believe there is a place waiting for me: Heaven. A setting at His table. A place in His Kingdom, just for me. Gives me hope for tomorrow. I wake up with a smile on my face each morning, and I like it.

I am known as the 'lady who prays' and gives hugs to EVERYONE. (Giving away God's love! the coolest part is that I get it right back!) My desire is to shine like Jesus and be the female version of Jesus himself. So, when you see me, you see Jesus. You see *LOVE.*

I have established a relationship with my daughter and even play a part in my grandchildren's lives. Several times a week, I am responsible for picking them up from school and dropping them off at home. There are times that I get to have them overnight or even for the weekends. It is very rewarding. And it is a lot easier when I have love in my heart and I am sober. They certainly don't need a drunken gramma in their precious young lives.

I am still working on a relationship with my son. That may take some time. God is at work on this. I believe, and I am hopeful. I am a child of God. A daughter of a King. I am royalty. And so are you, if you believe. My purpose is to love, ALWAYS. It is so easy to do and doesn't cost a thing. I dare you to try it.

CHAPTER 29

DID YOU KNOW?

Would you like to know some truth? You were born a winner! Yes, YOU! All of us were. Yes, ALL of us.

God designed us all as His precious and beloved children. He doesn't make mistakes. You are intentional. And you matter to Him. He created you, *specifically, a*nd wants you to be His child. He wants to add YOU to His family. He sees you and believes in YOU. He needs you to know that YOU ARE NOT ALONE. HE IS WITH YOU. AND HE IS WAITING FOR YOU.

His plan for you is greater than anything you can possibly imagine, because it is of Him, and each and every one of us has a purpose. His purpose. NOT yours. NOT mine. We all need to make His will, Our will. And we need to choose Him. First and foremost, AND ALWAYS.

It's your choice that He gave to you. Free will. Now, what do you do with it? SEEK HIM. He is the **ONLY** way to become who you were meant to be and become **truly** free!!!!

Let Him in. Let Him guide you. He will. He will do all the hard work and always does a great job! Lean into Him and see how strong you feel. It's MAGNIFICENT! We may be broken, but we don't have to stay that way. Find Jesus, and you will NEVER be the same. HE IS EMPOWERING. What do you have to lose?

CHAPTER 30

THE END

So, I've been trying to figure out how to end this book, but I have realized there is NO ending. Because **God is still writing my story.** If I haven't bored you with this story of growth, then tune in for what's to come. I'll share with you the signs and wonders and the visions and 'glimmers' that God has given to me.

My journey with Jesus is FAR from over! Until we meet again... I will shine Jesus for all to see.

God BLESS

Once wicked, now God's warrior.

THANK YOU

Thank You, God, for all that You do for me. For ALWAYS being there for me, even when I didn't know it. Thank You for sticking around when You didn't have to. Thank You for believing in me and NEVER giving up on me! Thank You for making a way when I couldn't see any way possible. Thank You for forgiving me of my sins EVERY DAY. (I am not perfect by any means!)

Thank You for ALWAYS providing for me, whether it be financial, emotional, spiritual, or physical. You ALWAYS have my back. Thank You for giving me such wonderful and loving people in my life. I know You placed each one with great intentions to be excellent role models, and they are succeeding beyond their gifts and talents.

Thank You for the family I have been given: my Moms and Pops. They invite me into their lives without hesitation and with the greatest love I have ever known. Thank You for restoring my relationships with my children. I know there is still a long road to recovery in this department, but I KNOW You are at work... ALWAYS. Even when I can't see it or feel it. You are working. And it is ALWAYS for my good.

Thank You for choosing me and adding me to Your Family! And Thank You, most of all, for Your LOVE. Your undeniable LOVE. It saved me. You saved me.

Thank You, God, for this journey. I could have NEVER done this on my own. GRATEFUL!

Thank you to all the Pastors who gave me hope and believed in me.

Thank you to all my brothers and sisters along the way, who gave me strength and encouragement.

Shout out to my girls, Deb O, Pam K, Sharon M, & Liann K

I am becoming the person I am supposed to be because you all believed in me, encouraged me, and loved me unconditionally! I ABSOLUTELY LOVE YOU ALL.

Thank you to all the churches in this wonderful, WONDEROUS way.

To my children and grandchildren, my hope is that I leave you with a better vision of myself and greater memories to come. Thank you for all your love. So, looking forward to the next chapters of our lives. I believe it will be MORE than awesome! I LOVE Y'ALL!

If I have failed to mention anyone who has traveled this road of recovery with me, it was and is NOT intentional.

My sincerest apologies. And THANK YOU!

*Once again, **THANK YOU GOD, FOR ALL THAT YOU DO FOR ME. I LOVE YOU. I AM YOURS AND YOU ARE MINE.***

FOR ALL OF ETERNITY.

I AM TRULY BLESSED.

Yes, and Amen.

ACKNOWLEDGEMENT

I received an email from my church requesting help for a lady in need. I was then asked by someone if there was any way I could help her. I observed her in church as a new participant. Thought to myself, this is one person to stay away from. Then I received a request from a friend if I could help her. I talked to my wife, Sharon, and decided that the third time confirmed that the Lord wanted me to help her, ugh. Positioned her trailer in my back yard and set it up. Boy, was I wrong about her. She seemed to genuinely have a desire to follow Jesus. She has become a real blessing for me. Her enthusiasm for Jesus has been very refreshing, it is not fake. My wife and I have informally adopted this 55 year old child. The situations she has included in this book are not all conclusive, there is more. She is proof that your situation can change if you want it bad enough. I believe the Lord has big things planned for this Christs warrior.

Mike Lee (Dad)

54773343R00048